# THE *mini* T-RRIBLE

## BY J.N. PAQUET

One day, a funny looking object landed on the grass, in a swishy sound. *SWISH SWISH… SWISH SWISH…*

A tiny two mouth monster jumped off the spaceship.
His name? *The T-RRIBLE!*

After his long space travel, the little monster really needed exercising. *Arms up, arms down… To the left, to the right… Jump up, jump up…*

*The T-RRIBLE* then walked on the wetly muddy soft grass.
SMUSHY-SMUSH! SMOOSHY-SMUSH! SMISHY-SMUSH!

Walking in the streets of the big city, he saw a rather strange three eyed creature and asked an old lady: *"Excuse me. What is this thing, please?"*

*"The traffic lights, my little cream cheese!"* She answered with a smile. But when she saw him, she got so scared she ran away, screaming: *"Monster! Monster!"*

*The T-RRIBLE* then walked again a bit until he stopped at a little house. He knocked at the door. *KNOCK KNOCK…*

A smiling little boy called Oliver Bluemoon and his mummy opened the door. *"I've got some T-RRIBLE news!"* The little monster shouted. *"An asteroid will destroy my planet! Only YOU can save us!"*

"*I am too small!*" Oliver replied. "*You are special because you speak two languages!*" The T-RRIBLE explained. "*On my planet, T-RRIBLE 4, nobody speaks two languages!*"

*"You are really special to us! Please, come with me to my planet."*
With a YES from his mummy, Oliver gladly accepted.

In the garden, the two new friends stood in a puddle.
*The T-RRIBLE* placed a stone on Oliver's left hand and said:
*"Close your eyes. Think about the stars and let the stone fall."*

A door appeared. *"It is a shortcut, a passage to my planet. We can only use it once, it is a secret!"*
Then, they stepped through the door.

They landed on *T-RRIBLE 4*, a green planet with clouds and fields, two rivers and honey trees everywhere.
And plenty of little monsters running, running, running…

*"We must hurry!"* *The T-RRIBLE* said. The two little friends ran through the green cotton grass, to meet with *King ADO-RABLE,* who they found crying, on his own, in a walkway. Everyone had left the castle.

*"Your Majesty, my friend Oliver will help us. He speaks two languages!"* The King explained that the Dark King, from the other land, didn't speak his language.
*"Let's go to see him!"* Oliver said.

Whilst climbing the mountain to the dark side of the planet, Oliver taught his two little companions some words in the other King's language: *"'Bonjour' means 'Hello' and 'Merci' means 'Thank you.'"* They loved it!

In the dark palace, they found *King HO-RRIBLE* all alone, staring at the sky. *« Qui êtes-vous? »* He blasted.
*"Who are you?"* Oliver translated.

Oliver explained to the two Kings how they had to work together to save their planet: *"If both your lasers hit the asteroid at the same time, you will stop it."* They agreed and shook hands.

When the clock struck nine, the two lasers finally hit the rock and… diverted it, as expected!
*"We did it!"* The T-RRIBLE screamed, jumping around.

To thank Oliver for his precious help, the two Kings gave a big party in his honour where honey was flowing like water.
Everyone was celebrating the happy ending.

As it was time to go, the two Kings promised everyone would soon learn the two languages. Then, with a chalk, *The T-RRIBLE* drew a door on a wall. A passage to Earth this time. *"See you soon, my friend!"*

Oliver stepped through the magical door and found himself back home, in his room, a few minutes before.
*"Was that all just a dream?"* The little boy wondered.

Suddenly the bell rang at the door. Oliver ran down the stairs, hoping to meet his friend again. Alas, no monster.
But a medal with an engraved… number 4!

**FROM THE SAME AUTHOR:**

OVER 50 BOOKS IN MONO, BILINGUAL & TRILINGUAL FORMATS
AVAILABLE AT: WWW.JNPAQUET-BOOKS.COM

THE BOOK OF THE ANIMALS (7 Books)
THE BOOK OF THE ANIMALS – mini (x7)
THE BOOK OF THE ANIMALS – COLLECTION (x3)
THE BOOK OF THE ANIMALS – SPECIALS (x3)
THE BOOK OF THE ANIMALS – SPIN-OFF (x4)
THE BOOK OF THE ANIMALS – COLOURING TOGETHER (x2)

HAPPY LITTLE LUKA (x2)

I JUST LOVE MONSTERS!
I JUST LOVE MY FRIENDS!
I JUST LOVE DINOSAURS!

MELY & BELA IN THE KINGDOM
OF THE BLUE STRAWBERRIES

WHEN EVERYTHING IS... LITTLE AND BLUE

MY FIRST SMARTBOOK

LITTLE CHARLIE VISITS LONDON

WAKEY WAKEY!

THE T-RRIBLE (x2)
THE mini T-RRIBLE (x2)

PRINCE GEORGE: NO BATH ON A MONDAY!

ONCE UPON A TOUR

JACOB & DAD – HUG IT OUT!

BABIES' DREAMS

This book is dedicated to Isabela, Amélie & Alex.

Copyright © 2013-2015 J.N. PAQUET. Characters, text & illustrations copyright.

The right of J.N. PAQUET to be identified as the Author of the Work has been asserted by him in accordance with the Copyright, Designs and Patent Act 1988. All rights reserved. No part of this publication may be reproduced, stored in a retrieval system, or transmitted, in any form or by any means without the prior written permission of the author, nor be otherwise circulated in any form of binding or cover other than that in which it is published and without a similar condition being imposed on the subsequent purchaser. To publish, republish, copy or distribute this book, please contact: contact@jnpaquet-books.com

"The T-RRIBLE" and JNPAQUET Books Ltd Publishing Rights © J.N. PAQUET.

"The T-RRIBLE" characters, names and related indicia are © 2013-2015, J.N. PAQUET - All rights reserved.

Copyright © 2015, JNPAQUET Books Ltd. All rights reserved. Special Edition.

J.N. PAQUET™ is a trade mark registered in the UK Register of Trade Marks, in the United Kingdom, under No. 2540865

ISBN 9781910909324 (PAPERBACK)
eISBN 9781910909331 (EBOOK)

www.ingramcontent.com/pod-product-compliance
Lightning Source LLC
Chambersburg PA
CBHW081130080526
44587CB00021B/3823